# The J.J. Johnson Collection

**ARTIST TRANSCRIPTIONS — TROMBONE**

Transcribed by Scott Whitfield

Cover photo courtesy of MICHAEL OCHS ARCHIVES / Venice, CA

ISBN 0-7935-5750-X

7777 W. BLUEMOUND RD. P.O. BOX 13819 MILWAUKEE, WI 53213

Copyright © 1996 by HAL LEONARD CORPORATION
International Copyright Secured   All Rights Reserved

For all works contained herein:
Unauthorized copying, arranging, adapting, recording or public performance is an infringement of copyright.
Infringers are liable under the law.

# The J.J. Johnson Collection

| | |
|---|---|
| 8 | *Azure* |
| 10 | *Bloozineff* |
| 18 | *Blue Nun* |
| 20 | *Coffee Pot* |
| 24 | *Concepts in Blue* |
| 26 | *Deak* |
| 28 | *Fatback* |
| 13 | *Flat Black* |
| 32 | *In Walked Horace* |
| 35 | *Jevin* |
| 38 | *Lament* |
| 40 | *Me Too* |
| 46 | *Mellodee* |
| 49 | *Nermus* |
| 52 | *Night Flight* |
| 55 | *Opus De Focus* |
| 58 | *Pinnacles* |
| 66 | *Shutterbug* |
| 70 | *Sidewinder* |
| 74 | *Smoky* |
| 76 | *Turnpike* |
| 80 | *Turnpike* (Alternate Take) |
| 61 | *Wee Dot* |
| 84 | *Why Not* |

Star Line Productions

# J.J. Johnson

is often cited by historians as the most important trombonist in the post-war era of jazz. His remarkable technical fluency and improvisational skill has made him a living legend. He has influenced many trombonists over the years, and his composing and arranging talent is respected and admired by his fans and colleagues alike.

James Louis Johnson was born in Indianapolis, Indiana in 1924. He studied the piano when he was nine, and started playing trombone when he was fourteen. By the age of seventeen, he was on the road playing in the Clarence Love and 'Snookum' Russell territory big bands. He joined the Benny Carter orchestra in 1942, and composed music for the band. One of his pieces, "Polishin' Brass", was featured on a radio broadcast to servicemen overseas. He was a member of the Count Basie band from 1945, and wrote the classic "Rambo" during his several months in the trombone section. He made New York his home in 1946, and played in various jazz groups on 52nd Street during the classic years of the bebop era. He performed and recorded with Charlie Parker, Dizzy Gillespie, Fats Navarro, Miles Davis, Bud Powell, and Max Roach. By 1952, however, lack of steady work forced him to take a job with the Sperry Gyroscope Company as a blueprint inspector.

In August, 1954, he was back on the scene with a new group co-led by trombonist Kai Winding. Their appearances and recordings set the jazz world on its ear. Unfortunately, the group disbanded in 1956. J.J. put together a new quintet, as well as fulfilling several commissions for compositions. His "Poem For Brass" from 1956 was well received by critics and audiences, as well as two works for the 1959 Monterey Jazz Festival, "El Camino Real" and "Sketch For Trombone And Band." In 1961, a large work for Dizzy Gillespie, "Perceptions", was recorded for Verve Records.

Throughout the sixties, he played in various combos, and led a sextet with Clark Terry and Sonny Stitt that toured Japan in 1964. However, by the late '60s, J.J. was spending most of his time writing commercial music. In 1970, he moved to Los Angeles to write music for film and television; one of his first credits was orchestrating and arranging parts of Isaac Hayes' score for "Shaft".

By the late '80s, he was back to playing jazz full time. In 1995, he realized a long-standing dream of recording with the legendary arranger/conductor Robert Farnon. The resulting album, "Tangence", was very well received.

He currently lives in Indianapolis, playing better than ever, and composing new music for upcoming concerts.

MICHAEL OCHS ARCHIVES / Venice, CA

# Selected Discography

| Title | Year | Label/Cat. No. |
|---|---|---|
| The Eminent Jay Jay Vol 1 | 1953 | BLP 1505 |
| The Eminent Jay Jay Vol 2 | 1953 | BLP 1506 |
| Four Trombones | 1953 | Prestige PRCD-24097-2 |
| The Eminent Jay Jay Johnson | 1954 | Blue Note BLP 1505 (LP)<br>Blue Note CDP 7-81506-2 (CD) |
| Really Livin' | 1959 | Columbia CL 1383 |
| J.J. Inc. | 1960 | Columbia PC 36808 |
| A Touch Of Satin | 1960 | Columbia CL 1737 |
| Betwixt and Between | 1968 | A & M SP 3016 |
| The Yokohama Concert | 1977 | Pablo 2620-109 |
| Pinnacles | 1979 | Milestones M 9093 |
| Concepts in Blue | 1980 | Pablo 2312-123 |
| Vivian | 1992 | Concord-Jazz 4523 |
| Let's Hang Out | 1992 | EmArcy 314-514454-2 |
| Tangence | 1994 | Verve 314-526-588-2 |

# AZURE

Trombone

By J.J. Johnson

# BLOOZINEFF

Trombone

By J.J. Johnson

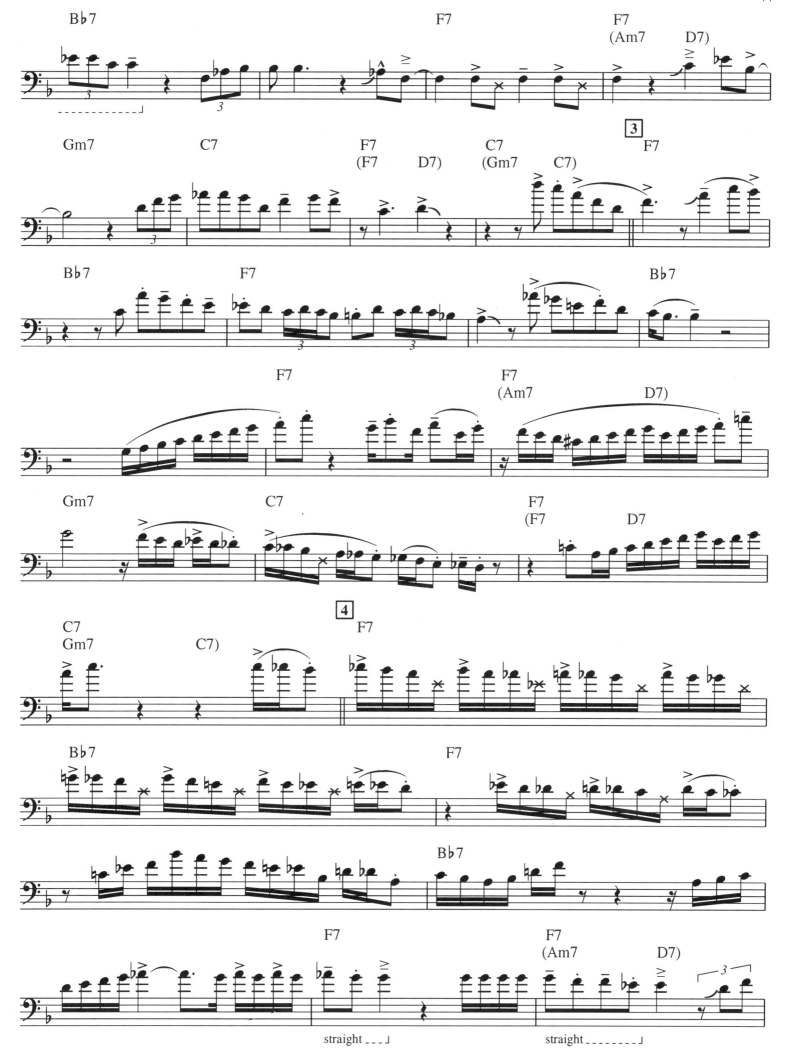

# FLAT BLACK

Trombone

By J.J. Johnson

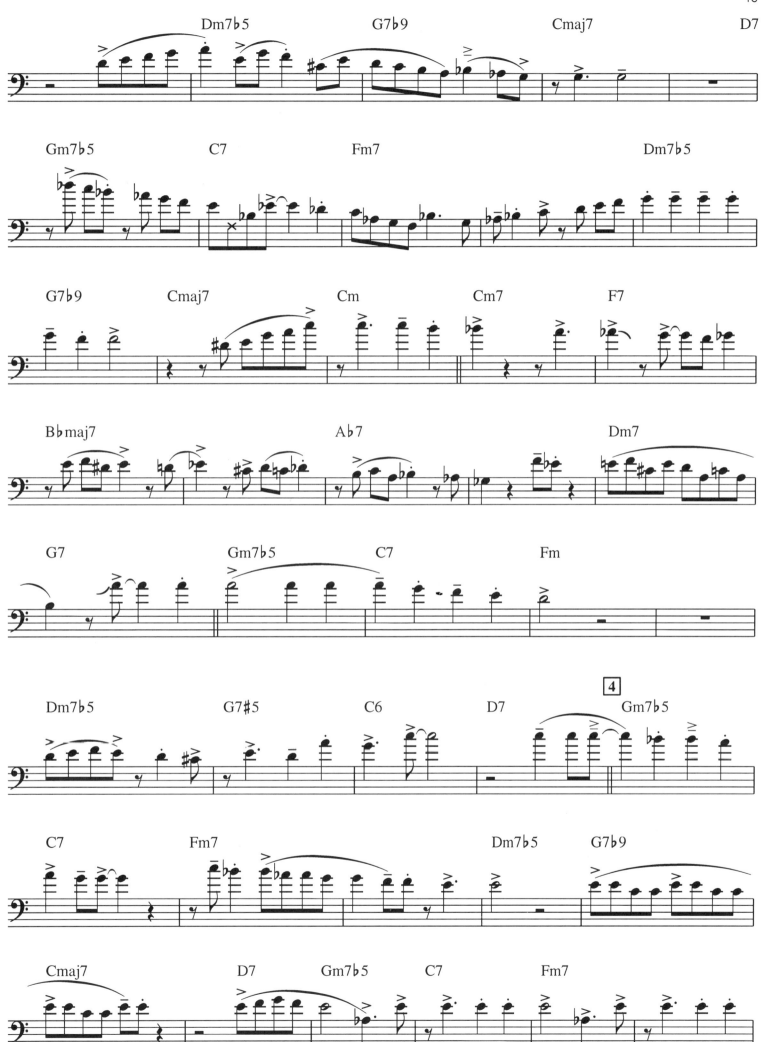

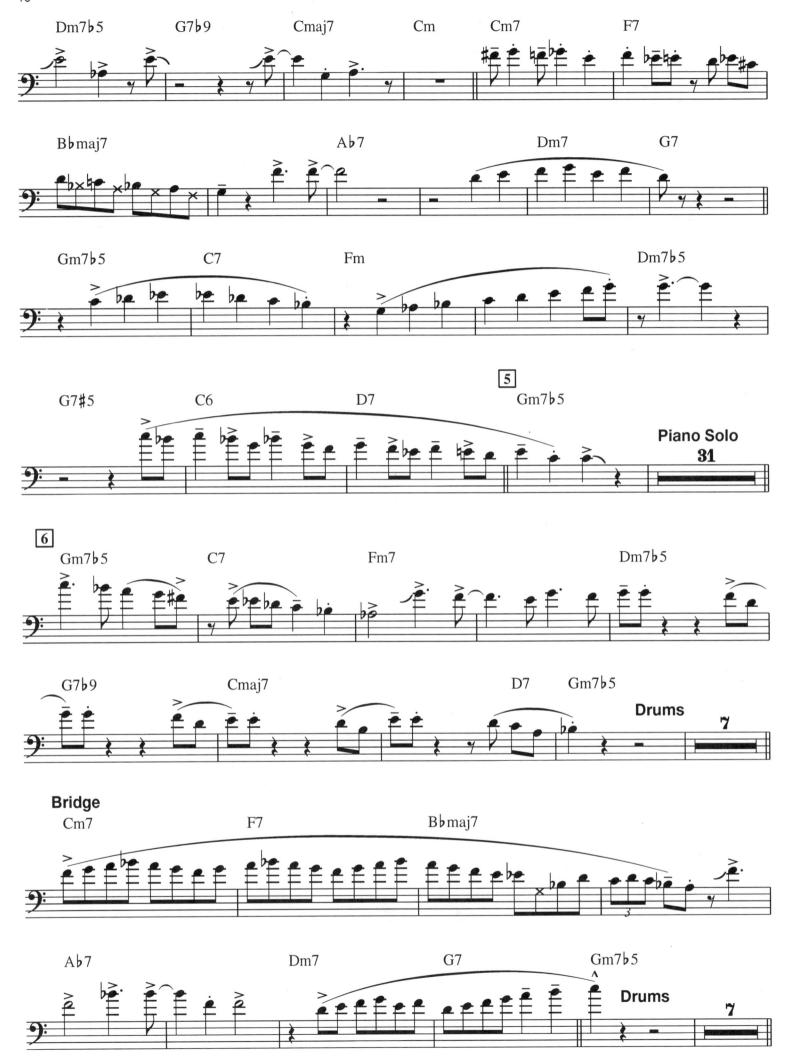

# BLUE NUN

By J.J. Johnson

# COFFEE POT

Trombone

By J.J. Johnson

# CONCEPTS IN BLUE

Trombone

By J.J. Johnson

# DEAK

**Trombone**

By J.J. Johnson

Medium (♩ = 132)

# FATBACK

Trombone

By J.J. Johnson

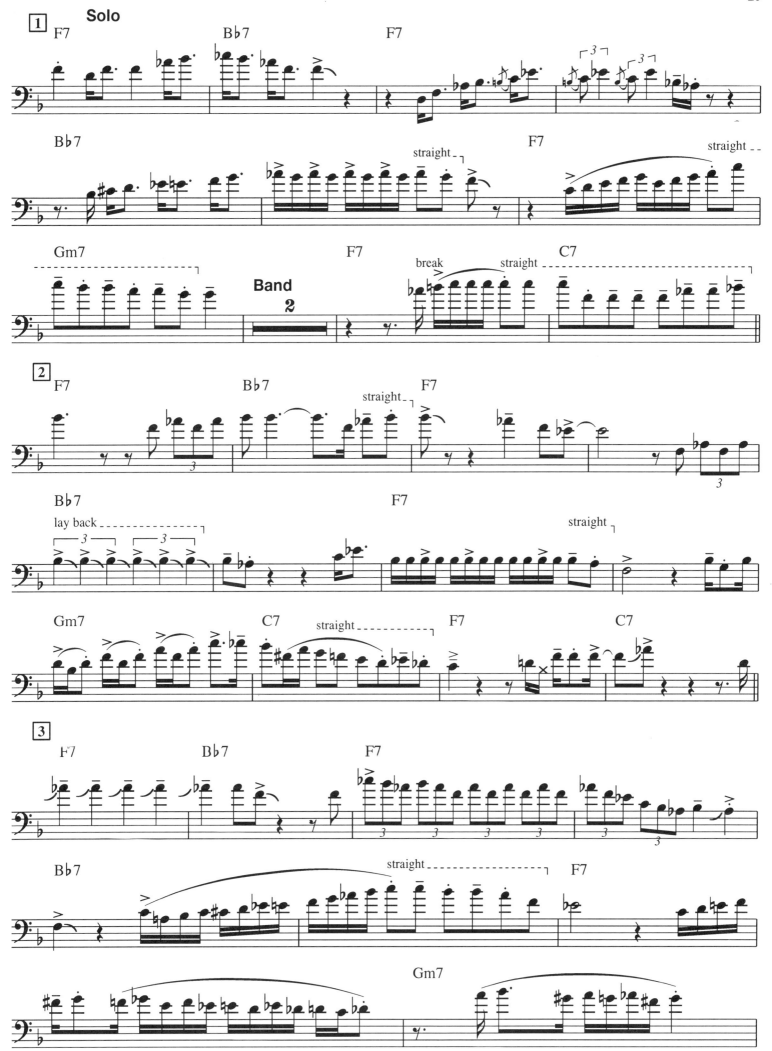

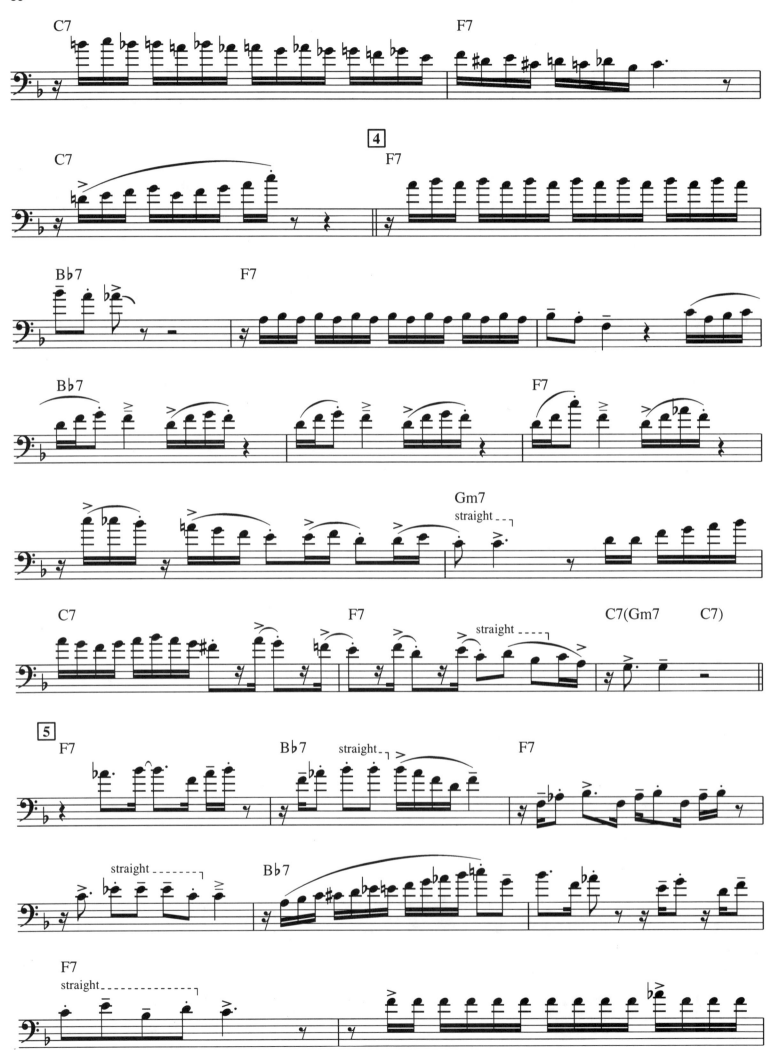

# IN WALKED HORACE

Trombone

By J.J. Johnson

# JEVIN

Trombone

By J.J. Johnson

Fast Waltz (♩. = 98)

# LAMENT

Trombone

By J.J. Johnson

# ME TOO

**Trombone**

By J.J. Johnson

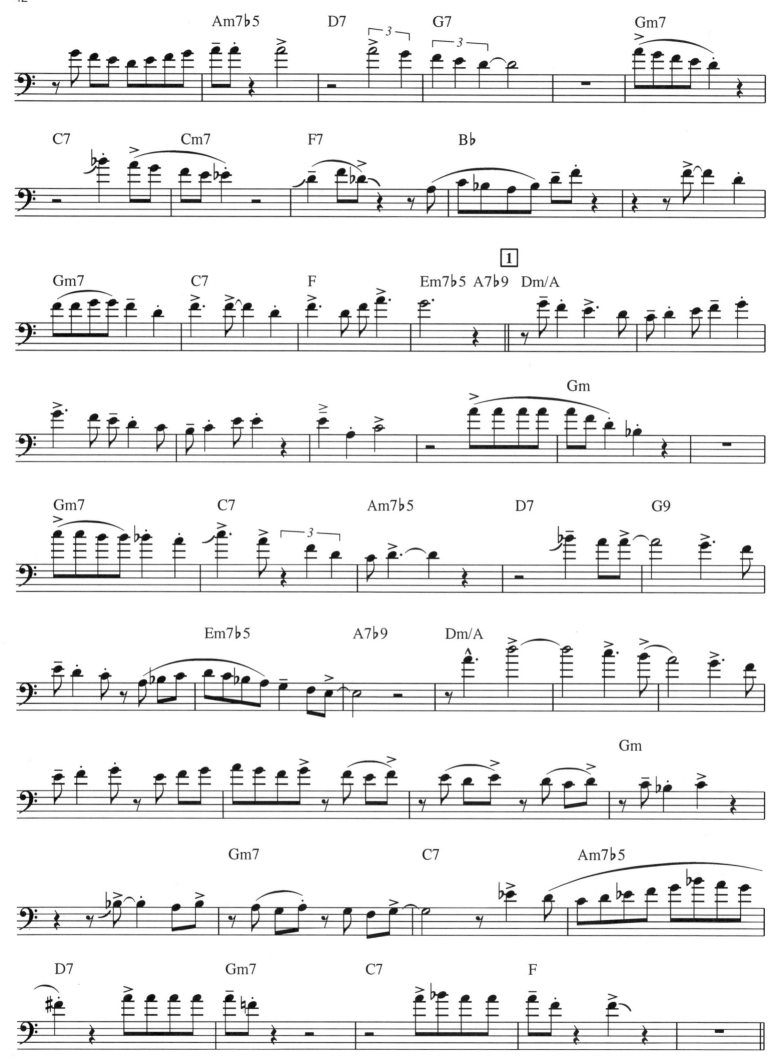

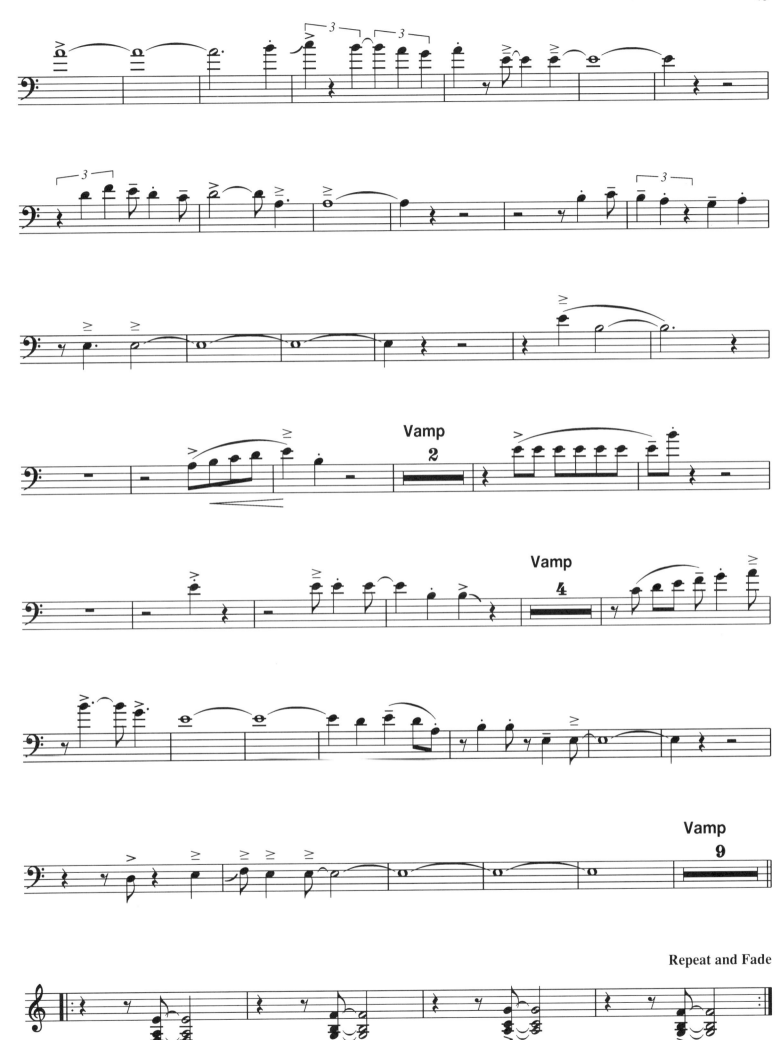

# MELLODEE

Trombone

By J.J. Johnson

# NIGHT FLIGHT

By J.J. Johnson

# OPUS DE FOCUS

Trombone

By J.J. Johnson

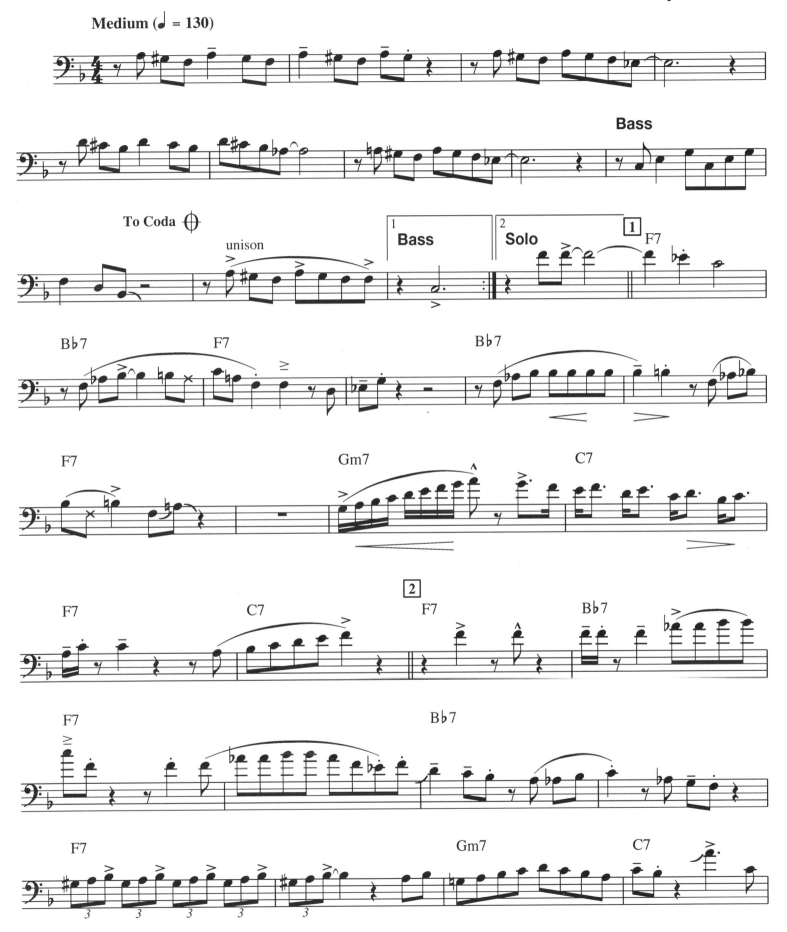

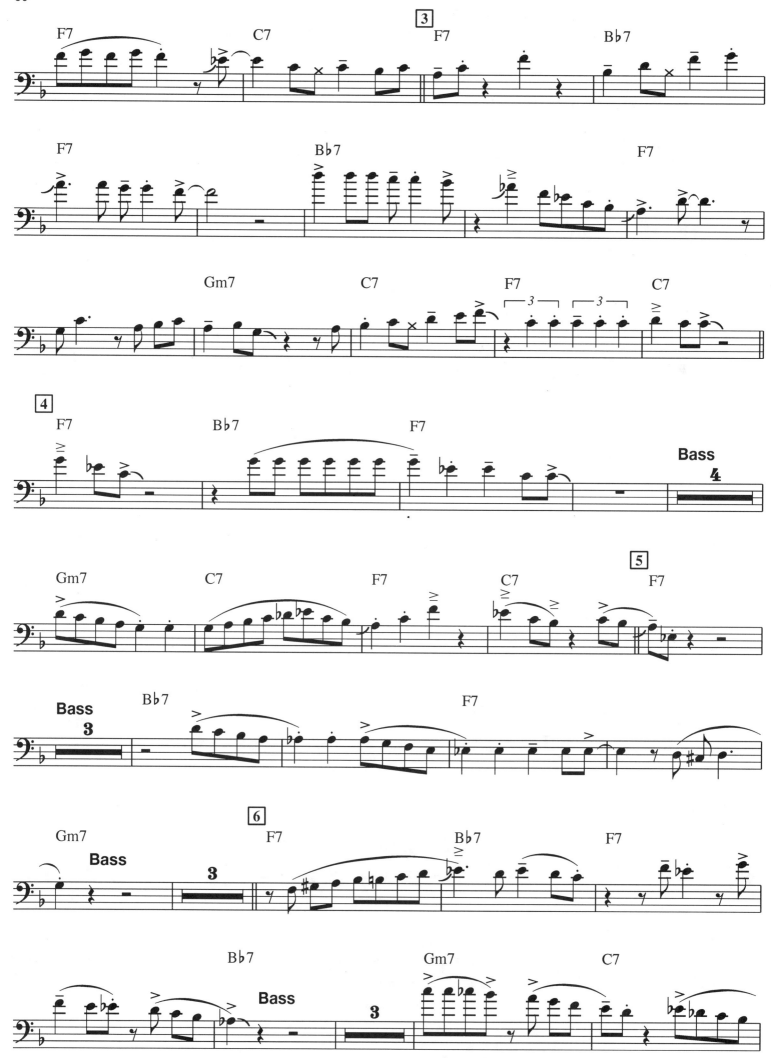

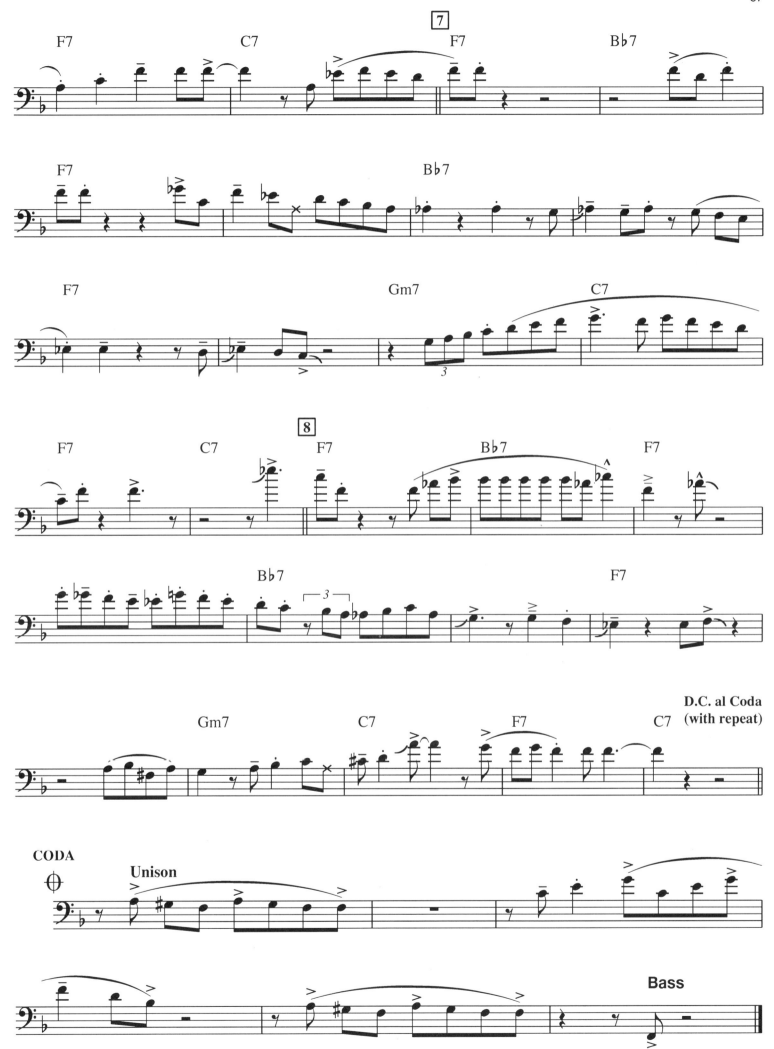

# PINNACLES

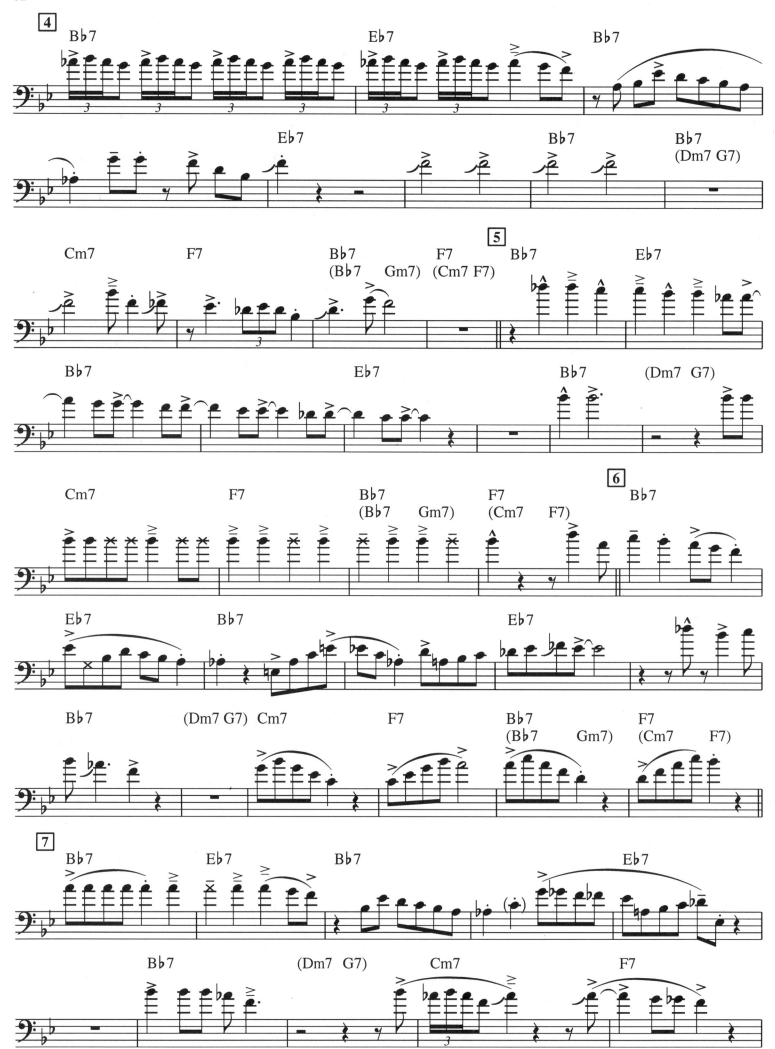

# SHUTTERBUG

Trombone

By J.J. Johnson

Copyright © 1960 TWO JAYS PUBLISHING CO.
Copyright Renewed
International Copyright Secured   All Rights Reserved

# SIDEWINDER

Trombone

By J.J. Johnson

Copyright © 1959 TWO JAYS PUBLISHING CO.
Copyright Renewed
International Copyright Secured  All Rights Reserved

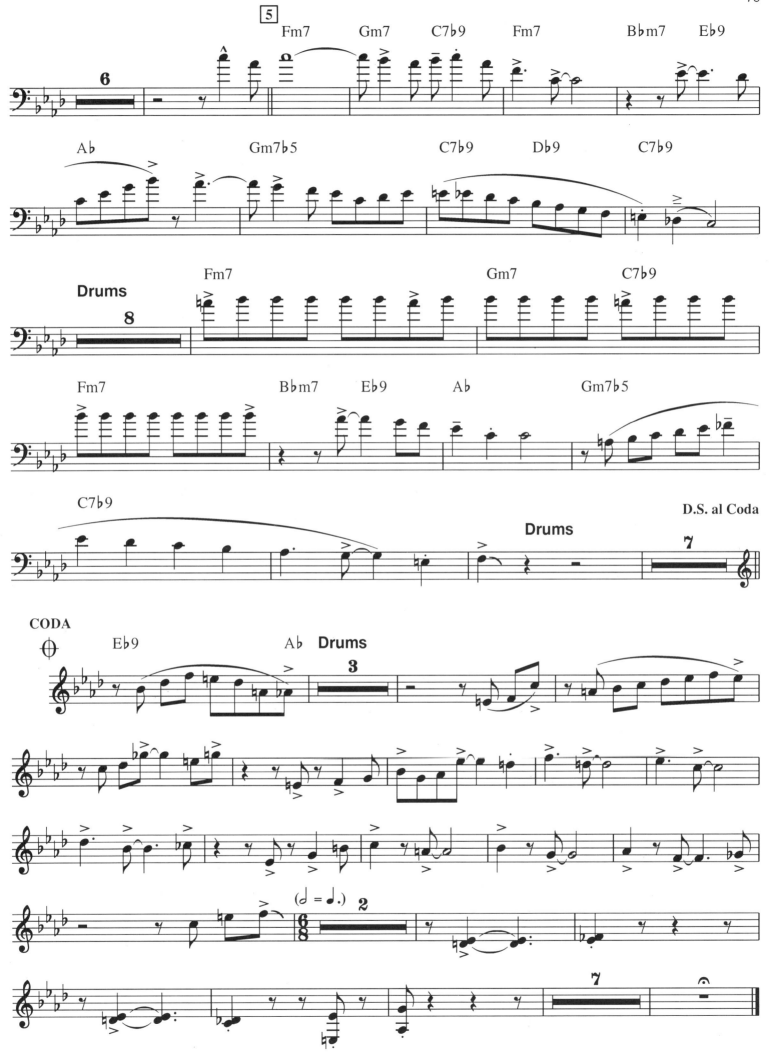

# SMOKY

By J.J. Johnson

# TURNPIKE

Trombone

By J.J. Johnson

Copyright © 1953 (Renewed 1981) by MJQ Music, Inc.
International Copyright Secured   All Rights Reserved

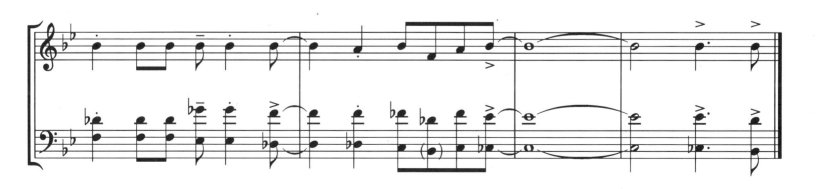

# TURNPIKE
## Alternate Take

Trombone

By J.J. Johnson

Copyright © 1953 (Renewed 1981) by MJQ Music, Inc.
International Copyright Secured   All Rights Reserved

83

Drum Solo

Bass Solo